Sue

with best

Winter River

David Whitwell

STEPHEN MORRIS

For Alex, Lauren, Winston, Theo, Mostyn and Benjamin

First published in 2021 by Stephen Morris
www.stephen-morris.co.uk
smc@freeuk.com

© David Whitwell e: davidwhitwell2@gmail.com

ISBN 9781838472627

British Library Cataloguing-in-Publication Data
A catalogue record for this book is available from the British Library

Design and typesetting © Stephen Morris 2021
set in Hoefler Text 10/13.5

Contents

Acknowledgements

Thanks to David Cook, Matthew Barton and Philip Lyons who encouraged me to start writing poems in the first place, and then kept me at it.

The Lansdown Poets have been a very positive and friendly group of poetry enthusiasts, year in year out.

Particular thanks to Philip for helping me put this collection together and to Stephen Morris for his patient editing.

Birdsong

Nesting in the eaves outside my window
the birds started up way before the dawn.
They were close and very loud:
they were shouting.

Coming back from London
to our home by the river,
I used to complain about the birds.

That chorus was always a surprise
welcoming me back,
to my childhood home.
I loved it,
but because I sometimes complained,
it became a family joke.
Those birds, camped outside my room,
were a sign,
that this was the real life:
there all the time,
waiting for my return.
I've never heard such a noise in the early morning.
Did I imagine it?
Were my young ears too sensitive?
If I went back now,
to that room under the eaves,
would I hear it again?
No, I remember now,
it is all gone
that house is no more.

Detachment

I remember the old rectory,
where I went as a child
to play with Peter – the Rector's son.
There were endless empty attics
where we charged about playing hide and seek.
After that, clergymen
always seemed quite friendly;
but our family were unbelievers.
Religious persons
were regarded as figures of fun.

You could say we were bigotted,
an intolerant little sect,
and it went further:
we didn't like politicians either.
There was a boundary round our house
and the real world
was inside.
I wouldn't call it a handicap
but it led to a certain detachment,
a separation from things
others find important.

On Halkyn Mountain

When we went prospecting –
no, much too grand a term:
we were just amateurs.
When we went looking for minerals,
galena was like gold to us.
If we searched all day
we'd find a few bits.
Wonderfully heavy in the hand,
broken open with a hammer,
it shone – sparkling in the sunlight.

One time on Halkyn Mountain,
nosing about in old workings
we found a train,
abandoned when the mine closed.
Trucks tumbled over broken tracks
lying full of weeds,
birch trees growing through rusty iron.
This scared us
we knew we were trespassing
but the tunnel entrance drew us in.
Looking around the fallen wagons
we found great lumps of ore.
We filled our bags
and set off down the mountain
but struggling now.
Why did we need so much?
We set it down
most got left behind.

For years that scene played on:
a kind of grief at lost desire.
We'd found so much,
more than we had dreamt of.
Couldn't we still
make something of it?
But the lust was gone
it was just rock:
there was no going back.

Acrocorinth

We got to Corinth in time for supper
goat stew with beans and olives,
and wine laced with turpentine.
All so good, we were inspired,
got the idea to spend the night
in the ancient citadel, high above.
So up the cliffs, into the dark
we struggled on through bramble and thorn
and found a place at the very top,
inside the walls of the ruined town.
Exhausted by our day in the sun
we lay flat out,
laughed at what we'd done.
Looked up at the stars
and The Milky Way
was a bright silver band
across the sky.
And shooting stars we saw a few
then more and more
until it seemed
the skies were falling
before our eyes.

April 13th 2016

A lift to the airport, making good time,
fuss with security soon overcome.
Coffee at Starbucks, waiting for the gate.
Things going well, this is the life
We'll be there for lunch
in the south of France.

A call on the mobile, *Admitted to hospital*.
Something gone wrong, way before time.
Have to get out, go back through the system,
a bus to the city retracing our steps.
Walking through streets, with baggage in tow,
it feels unreal,
strange to be here.

A long wait for news through a hot afternoon.
The season was changing, spring bursting forth.
All life advancing but ours standing still. Then
just after six they said it had happened.
At seven we visited – wonderful sight.
A mother in triumph
the baby doing fine.
And no one had guessed
that his name would be Winston.

Last Lunch with Eileen

The light on the levels surprised us
that last time.
Unexpectedly bright with
all the colours of early summer.
Driving to The Inn at Burtle
we saw swans on the bank
and ducks swimming in the rhyne.

A hot wind was blowing from the Mendips,
not cooling us at all
just rattling the awning
over where we sat.

You were talking about life in Burma,
gentle people you remembered so well.
You had told me about them before.

The girl who brought our lunch delighted you
with her manners and her looks.
She was from Poland.
So nice you said.

After all your long journeys,
this was it. You were 96.
Nothing else happened that last day.
It was hot and you were on good form,
still had time for a slow lunch with your nephew.
You had some beer and a pudding,
said it was all perfect,
you couldn't eat more.
You were so bright that day.

The Empire

Mr Brown taught us French:
he was a smooth man, who always wore a suit.
And when he supervised lunch
he made it an occasion.
Lectured us on how to hold our forks.
Said it could make all the difference
when we were being considered
for the governorship of some distant province.

We knew about the Empire
from the roll of honour on the wall.
Generations of boys had gone out,
that's what we were meant to do.
To Somaliland, Uganda, Singapore.
Malaya, Rhodesia, Hong Kong.

There were books in the library
we looked at on wet afternoons.
Far away places, people and customs.

My lot never got there.
The wind changed before we were ready.
Overnight, all swept away,
the names disappeared from the map.
The Friendly Islands, Burma, Nyasaland,
The Gold Coast, Tanganyika, Ceylon.
Just knowing those names makes me part of it.

And now the Empire is back
but what we once thought so special
is being called an abomination.

Got me thinking about Mr Brown and that roll of honour,
and us growing up under the old dispensation.
It's gone now, just as surely,
as when the Romans left these shores.
And the story being told
and who is telling it
will be changed forever.

At the Hot Gates

The War crippled me chiefly because it was something
I was neither honestly in nor honestly out of
  TS Eliot August 1929

I also was never at the *Hot Gates*,
nor knee deep in the salt marsh, heaved a cutlass.
My whole generation,
were kept away from armed conflict.
Not for us the breaking of spirits that was Vietnam.
We weren't made to do anything.

At the real Thermopylae,
Leonidas, King of Sparta, facing certain defeat,
died for the glory of his people
I was never asked to face anyone;
except maybe that chap, came in one day,
shouting the odds and waving a knife.
He gave it up without much trouble,
I think he just wanted to talk.
Otherwise nothing, zilch.
I go to my grave, sword undrawn.

Unless at this late stage,
anarchy finally takes over.
I have an old bayonet,
a souvenir my father brought from his war.
Could I learn to use it now?
It's still so sharp, (German manufacture).
Or would I go quietly, step aside,
give the mob what they want?

As a child we played war games all the time.
Rounding up the Jerries and the Japs,
shouting at them, shooting them.
I think at the last, up against a wall,
I'd be transported back.
Able to give free rein
to a justified hatred I've never known.
The thing that makes men
love war so much.

Boys

Sunday afternoons went on for ever,
hanging about, waiting.
In 1960 nothing ever happened.
It was so boring back then.

He was a misfit, my friend:
wouldn't comply or toe the line.
He enraged the masters,
the boys hated him,
a *pseudo-intellectual*,
and it was me
he taught so much.
The only one who would listen,
about God and the soul
and poems I never understood.
I could have followed his dangerous path
but I didn't have the nerve.

Sitting together one dull afternoon
he tapped my forehead,
and said in a funny voice,
Tell me what's in there.
What is it that makes you tick?
And I thought at once of the letter I was writing
to the girl from back home.
Those letters I wrote,
and the ones I received,
I realise now, they saved my life.
But I just smiled.
he never knew.

The Old Fellow

The old fellow came to talk to us.
Grey, distinguished and with a smile so warm
as though he had something special to tell us.
We were young, know nothing students,
and he had done everything:
soldier, publisher, prime minister.
I don't know why he bothered
but he really seemed to like us.
Such a long time ago, but even then
he said the world was too much.
We need a place that is safe,
secure from change and uncertainty,
people we know, really know,
and we need our families.
And there's the world of books
and gardens, people need gardens.
But apart from those things,
don't expect much when you go out there,
you are on your own.
And the things you will chase after, mean nothing,
give you nothing.

And then he was done, and later
I heard funny stories about him,
and his scandalous life.
But I know now he was right
about everything.

The Lonely Shore

the road sandy and full of holes
a Nissen hut
shy foreign faces smiling through the fence
smiling but not speaking
and then the shore
mile after mile

there was a rhythm to the days of solitude
the draw of that lonely place
life began on the shore
fragments driftwood   things washed up
crystals from the cliffs

unimaginable lives
a Nissen hut with faces at the window
foreign faces shy   not speaking
there behind a fence
the road sandy and full of holes

solitude started on the shore
walking alone
that was where my life began

Not getting across the Dee

Once I nearly made it across.
Wading thigh deep,
I reached the final channel,
just below the castle at Flint,
but then I lost my nerve.
Thought of the boys who drowned,
– I knew their names –
felt the sand shifting,
the current pulling me out to sea,
one slip and I'd be gone.

Turning back I knew
that's how a chance is lost.
I'll never know if I could have done it
or if a few more steps and I'd have drowned.
The wild remains unexplored –
and after that, always out of reach.

Attachment

If my world is safe:
if on the inside
it has always felt that way:
if I've been shielded from the worst,
then it was never of my doing.

If I have not starved,
nor slept in doorways on winter nights,
nor been assaulted,
nor wrongly imprisoned by corrupt officials,
I didn't achieve this for myself.

It was the women who did it.
They nourished me,
protected me.
I was nurtured by their gentle love
that is the bedrock of the world.

In the unfair division of spoils,
I'll never pay for what I got.

Lost

Like tears in rain.
So many stories will be lost,
things I've never told, never passed on.

Like the black jersey my mother knitted
when I was a skinny boy of just sixteen.
Had it in my rucksack
summer we hiked round Greece.
We boarded a ferry at Piraeus,
a little toy boat with funnel belching smoke,
deck covered in people all in black,
peasants with animals and children,
so much stuff no one could move.
We climbed a stack of life rafts
and slept there on the hard wooden boards:
I used that jersey to rest my head.
We woke in the dawn tied up in an unknown port.
In panic we asked the name,
they signalled no, it was not Heracleion.
Later, as the heat returned
we stopped again and they all surged off.
We jumped down, took our heavy packs
and set off into the morning.

That's where the jersey was lost,
up on the life raft: didn't miss it for days.
Maybe someone took it while I slept.
They were so suspicious,
thought we were Germans.
Or maybe someone found it, passed it on,

it would have fitted their scrawny bodies.
Someone could be wearing it still
– sixty years on.

She was not a great knitter – did it out of love,
the finest wool, the smallest needles.
It was a special present, fitted so well.
I must have told her I'd lost it,
but never really confessed how careless I was,
how much I took her love for granted.

Wallasey

Dying slowly,
my mother didn't want more treatment.
She had her bed brought downstairs
and lay all summer
watching her beloved river,
and the ever changing tides.

I had a new car that year, a Volvo estate,
she used to tease me about it.
One day she wanted us all to go for a drive,
she wanted to go to Wallasey.
As we set out she talked about it –
how they were living there, the year I was born.
This was all new to me –
going for a ride with my parents,
and talk about a place
she had never once mentioned, all my life.

When we got there my father named the street
and they tried to work out which had been their house.
Then my father said we should go round the corner
and find the place he had lived as a boy;
which he added,
was before most of the houses were built.
He talked about a pond where they caught sticklebacks.
Then we spoke about people building houses
in places where ponds had been.
There was another family – one I'd never heard of,
and an aunt who lived on the same street.

And why had we never come there before?
It was nearby,
not far from the place I had lived all my life.
I wanted to know so much,
but they laughed, they made light of it:
it was just a drive.
She liked the car, but still thought it funny.
We never talked about Wallasey again,
and that was probably the last time she left the house.

First Encounter 1958

Waking to shouts,
and a squeal of brakes,
the sign said Port Bou
we had arrived in Spain.
Blinded by the light
we stumbled over the tracks.
Heat, a smell of pine trees
and the wild sawing of cicadas:
first encounter with the South.

The old town, the castle, the cobbled streets,
flowers and palm trees,
and the sea, clear and alive.
We stayed for weeks,
got to know it so well,
the donkeys, the sardine boats,
and the Guardia Civil watching over us
with their guns and funny hats.
And around us, the cork forest,
twisted blackened trees clinging to the mountains.
We learned to live with the heat,
and the delicious cool of the evenings.

Casa Simeon in Tossa de Mar,
a little hotel on the Costa Brava.
How people used to sneer.
But it changed the world for ever:
something was hard-wired in.

By the Sea

Waste ground by a road in morning heat,
grass scorched by the sun,
rubble from a fallen wall,
yet a flower raises its head.

Racemes of yellow petals
on a thick juicy stem.
Just one flower, not fully out,
– an asphodel.

Death and the Elysian fields,
the mind scurries off,
sniffing out a classical allusion.
As though I was a poxy younger son,
off on the grand tour
showing off what I'd learnt at school.

And then I see they're everywhere.
Pushing up their heavy buds
on the cliffs,
out on the headland.
Tough succulent stems
bursting from the dusty ground.
Armies of them standing there,
far as the eye can see.

No need for all that ancient stuff,
here, in the fragrant south,
beside the iridescent sea.

Les Fauves

A sky like molten iron.
Boats signifying wealth and leisure.
Idleness seen in flashes of green.
The purple headland
for a future still possible.
Above the cerulean sea
that is the world within.
Patches of white
could be the houses on the bay
where you will never go.
Brush strokes
more vivid
more real
than life itself.

Elne

The place was closed, streets empty,
just one bar, with men outside.
The cathedral, on a great rampart,
massive, like a fortress.
A place to hide in time of trouble, you said,
as we looked for the way in.
Inside, stone columns rose in the darkness.
We struggled under the weight of it,
and the silence.
Brightness in the cloisters raised our spirits.
Amazing capitals
– fine example of something or other.
And from the roof terrace we could see,
it's a city built on a hill in a wide open plain,
mountains and sea way off in the distance.
Chosen as a safe place for its people
– but that was not to be.

When the town was stormed
they sought refuge inside.
But the doors were burnt off,
the women raped,
and everyone killed.
It was called the Martyr City
and it went on.
Elne changed hands many times.

Walking back through the silent town
it felt different.
It was Armistice Day,
rightly celebrated,
– but why so quietly?

Ripeness is All

I read of one, taken from happiness,
taken at the flood.
Loving husband and father,
swimming in the sea, when his heart gave out.
Not knowing the future, he'd left clothes on the beach.
Not knowing, he had plans for the afternoon.
His last view sinking down, a disc of sky refracted by waves.
Pale azure, almost white.
So unfair, he was not ready,
needed much more time.

He'd heard young fools say often enough,
better to die young.
To escape the grief that comes with age,
the embarrassment of slow decline.
Maybe he'd said such things himself,
but he needed time to recant.

As he lies down there with the fishes
it still looks so bright.
Though the distant sounds are fading now.
He knows it that moment,
the sweetness of the earth,
is all that there is.

He'd seen it in the morning,
sun on the roofs of the old town,
and the green of the trees,
where the mountains come down to the sea.
A place he could have lived
for as long as he was given.
He knows too late it's the greatest lie:
that he is going to a better place.

Sournia

Finding the house was easy.
We parked by the fountain with the Madonna,
and there it was, set behind its walls.
Way down south in the borderland, French Catalonia.
Under the dreaming peak of Canigó,
sacred mountain of Catalans.

She welcomed us in, told of her struggle;
how sad she was to leave:
back to Manchester and the grandchildren.
It was all there, all we could have wanted,
and the Mayor so welcoming:
Live with us, she said, *learn our ways*.

Lost in the hills,
a dry southern country of vines and olives;
the old frontier between France and Spain.
Such a garden of delight,
a grove of trees, an old ruin,
and terraces looking to the mountains.

Was it the final temptation:
one last not-to-be-repeated offer?
To chuck it all, and start again.
Leave the clouds and rain
make a new life in the sun.

But how to turn our backs
on all that we have been?
Become a foreigner, a Rosbif,
a tourist who just stayed on,
always such a long way from home.

Limoges

by Mr Silvero

With caressing hands, at Limoges
Who walked all night in the next room
  TS Eliot, *Gerontion*

Driving down France, the hour got late
we lost our way.
The towns had looked so welcoming
but in the dark there was nowhere to stay.
Then a sign to Limoges set me thinking
about Mr Silvero and his caressing hands.
walking all night in the room next door.
But who wants caressing hands these days
and what did it mean, anyway?

The streets were dark and empty
and at Hotel Boni they were closing up,
fended us off, said they were full.
But we were desperate so they let us in.
Up in the lift to the very last room
then we ate at La Vache au Plafond,
which means surprisingly
the cow on the ceiling.
Our room that night a soundproof box
then breakfast in Limoges and on our way.

There, in the dry season,
the Limoges of my mind,
with old Mr S next door.
So strange that all night long
we never heard a thing.

On a Beach

Near Cape Trafalgar, is
the best beach ever.
A clean sweep of sand,
umbrella pines on the hill,
and the glorious light of
the Costa de la Luz.

But there are sometimes bodies
found in the morning,
or boatloads of migrants scrambling ashore.
I may one day meet them
– as I sit there in the sun
drying after a swim.

Desperate people
in urgent need,
I'd have to help in some way
but I don't know what I'd do.
They'd want to get away
find a place they could hide
but though my car is just here
and I have a place in town,
would I really take them in?

Someone's sure to call the police,
who'll come and round them up,
while we tourists look away.

Then it's back to the little beach bar
to sit through the long light evening
while the sun sinks into the crystal sea.

Goat Years

Aphrodite – good name for a goat –
she was the queen of your heyday.
That's heyday with an e
nothing to do with hay – except...
that year John cut a path
through the long grass in the orchard
and we sat under the trees drinking wine.
It was too hot even there.
We had to go in under the thatch.

There were orphan lambs being reared on the bottle,
chickens roosting in the trees
and rabbits in the fields,
never seen so many rabbits.

Heyday *from an expression of joy or celebration* –
yet we never see it at the time.
Only, looking back it takes our breath away.

John made a cart for Aphrodite,
and the children had rides on the green.
There was lots of goats milk,
and kids born every year –
she went on and on.
It seemed that this was how life was
and she entered the record books
as the world's oldest goat.
But she got lame,
you didn't want to see her suffer.
The goat years were over.

John
i.m. John James 21.11.38 - 6.12.15

Deep in his lungs
long fibres of asbestos
buried their delicate crystals,
hiding for a lifetime.

Must have been in the engine room
in all that heat and noise
he breathed the dust.
Up the Amazon, round The Cape,
on to California –
all the world he travelled,
a Chief Engineer who saw it all.
So long ago it was forgotten –
until now.

The strongest, brightest man,
a boy at heart.
Always willing, able
to make things work,
John could solve any problem:
anything, he could repair.
He had no patience,
with things that didn't work.
A village man, he'd help anyone.
No time for fuss.

Half a century later
the fibres were still there.
He was struck down,
stuck on the ground,
waiting for a miracle.

Open Day

Open day at the vet school
There were cows and sheep
and donkeys we could ride.
There was food in the big house
but I never got that far.

So many things for us to see:
tumours, malformations,
and a calf born inside-out.
Then a man with rubber gloves
cutting through soft pink tissue,
fluid gushing out and
something inside I couldn't quite see.

Sweating and breathing hard
I wandered out to get some air,
and leaning against a wall,
slowly sank to the ground
where I lay looking up at fluffy white clouds,
and when I woke
I found I'd been sick.

So if I blanch and turn away
when you talk of cutting flesh,
it's a weakness covered up so long
I'd almost forgotten.
But now it comes back
with all these stories
of cutting little girls.

May Day

So many years dead, and still dead.
Always such a glorious day, this
May Day.
When every tree is covered and
all is hopeful for the coming.
So it's a big step to pass on,
never easy, since
there's no forgetting,
no let-up in regret.
Half a lifetime now
and still it goes on.

The Unexpected Guest

It was a surprise – alright a shock
that nearly killed me.
You, there, after all these years,
on the lawn afterwards.
Walking and talking with me and Willie:
just like we did in Heswall.

I knew you'd like it –
your sort of thing.
Old and young,
the sacred and the faintly ridiculous.
We stood by the ha ha, drinking,
soaking up the sun.

I should have introduced you to the bride,
she was only three, when you went away.
But you didn't want to cause a stir,
and I wasn't sure how to begin.

I know I've had it easy –
just happened that way.
You went away and I went on.
But I never forget what somebody said,
as we walked away outside the church,
that I *mustn't let it ruin the rest of my life* –
as though that was what I deserved.

You left the party before it got started,
the best was yet to come.
Why oh why
did you have to go?

The Job-thing

I bought a little saw, a pruning saw.
A luxury item really – Japanese.
It's very very sharp,
cuts as you pull towards you.
Small branches – it goes straight through,
for pollarding the willow – it was ideal.
Sounds like a dance
and it felt so good.
It's a job must be done
like shearing a sheep
to strengthen the trunk
stop it splitting in the wind.

Up the ladder, using that saw,
the thought occurred
I should have been a woodsman.
A man with strong hands
who knows the land.

Nothing like that was ever considered,
my career seemed to follow a pre-ordained path,
and a distant child I can hardly remember
decided early on the route it would take.

Some people change their job with ease
move on as soon as they've had enough.
The job-thing hardly touches them at all.
But for most of us it makes us
and shapes us
and we stick there to the end.

Sheds

They sort of crept up on me.
Years passed, decades, and all the time
small wooden buildings attracted me.
Thing was, I didn't really notice.
All those books with pictures and diagrams.
How to build your own shed.
And specialist fields, slate and metalwork
glass, electricity, insulation.
Then things got bigger:
log cabins, Alpine chalets,
medieval halls.

Looking back, someone should have said something.
It was the wood itself, the texture
the feel of it, the smell.
2x2, 2x4, 4x4, 6x6 ....
Then I met the family who own the saw mill
and they were so good
they would cut anything I wanted.
It started with pine, of course,
but moved on to oak and ash
and even some bits of elm they'd had for years.

I can see all my buildings now,
littered about,
but I think I may need one more.

At the End

Listen – here's another thing
for which I can find no name.

At the moment of crisis,
no, after that,
when things have been said
and there's no going back,
you've gathered your stuff
and you're leaving.
You've put it all in the car
and you look up
or you turn slightly – thinking,
this moment will not recur,
this is the end of all these things.
As you turn that last time
you find it's not what you thought,
it looks different.
There are doors you never entered,
windows you didn't know existed
and the face looking down
is not your old enemy
but someone once loved.

Maybe at the end,
it will be like this.
After all the things said
after letting go,
resigning to the flow running through you,
after it is too late for any response
maybe then you will see.

Free Will

If thoughts could break free
I could revisit some of the places
that left me wanting more.
Like the ruined nunnery
beside the Thames at Godstow.

I picture the nuns fishing in the river.
Maybe on hot days gathering up their skirts
and cooling their feet in the water,
where some passing monk or student might see them,
which maybe was their idea all along.
Which leads to thoughts of carnal knowledge
and the joy of movement:
knowledge that we are incarnate.

If our mind was really free
would it run on lines like these?

Being Alone

I got weary of the sheep
outside the house all day,
pulling on the grass
and in the night, coughing.
Always so sheep-like,
backing away from me, as though, I don't know,
as though I'm the intruder.
In the end I told him to put his sheep
somewhere else.
Up on the mountain, I don't care.
I prefer to be alone.

There's a feeling I once took for boredom,
an emptiness, a lack of urgency.
I am reduced to chopping wood for the fire,
cleaning the kitchen,
looking to the sky to see which way the clouds are going.
In the silence my thoughts become so loud,
conversations with the people I no longer see.
Rambling, one-sided.
I don't expect a reply
or that I will see them again,
but I can't escape the feeling
that they like to know what I'm doing.

The Trees

I'm neglecting the woods;
other madness has kept me away.
And now I forget even the seasons
and mislay the plans I made.
But in my absence the trees continue.

They don't need me.
All my efforts are
little more than random damage.
The scars soon heal –
it's I who need them.

The trees, in spite of all, will live on.
They are not tamed, though briefly
that seems to be the case.

Enduring love is not for the young.
Lust is what they need
to propagate and breed.

Love is what you're left with,
what you come back to,
like the trees.

The Tail

A previous life
now almost forgotten
trails along behind:
like the dangerous scaly tail
of an aging crocodile.

All those earlier incarnations,
still there,
out of sight.
So when you come forwards
as some new version of yourself
and you pause,
and turn a little to make a point,
the great scaly tail comes sweeping round
and all is chaos.

Apologise all you like
they'll never believe you didn't know
it was there behind you,
all the time.

Assessed under Section 136

at first tears   too angry to speak
irritated by my presence then fragments
a disjointed story   a world closing down
pain all around   like the headache I'm getting now
I can see you've no way out
no reason to go on living
and all that was left
was the hope you had of ending it all
I get it   I believe you
though I know you don't believe a word I say

and I ask myself again   why do this
put myself forward   pretending I can help
why should people go on living anyway
getting up   going to work   what is the point
there is no reason   no logic to it at all
it's an argument I cannot win

I see you're looking out of the window
do you know how useless I'm feeling now
you look at me for the first time and ask me what I do
do I often talk to people who just want to die

and it's a chink   you've invited me to talk
even saying I have no answer makes a bridge
reasoned arguments have failed
it's time to confess
I've nothing to set against the things you've told me
I can't persuade you of anything

and yet I have been down this way before
I've sat and listened head in hands eyes down
felt this bad thing in the room before
and then against the odds people survive
time makes a difference
allows new things to happen
I have seen many come back from this
so they can live again
don't know how don't know why
but it happens

this I do know

Summer Rain

Warm rain in August.
Heavy rain,
rushing off the roof and down the gurgling gutters.
Looking through the trees towards the old town,
houses misty under a warm haze.
Beautiful here in Clifton,
in England,
today,
the day the rains came.

Living here in the interstices,
hiding away from the world
among the hedges and sheds of city gardens.
Head well below the parapet,
savouring the smell of summer rain,
life is possible.
Indeed,
whisper it not abroad,
life is good.

The Chosen City

Weighed down by a year
of darkness and uncertainty,
we dash out to catch the sun
before it sinks into the west.
Out of breath we reach the top
as dazzling gold
lights up the Observatory
and a pink glow
shimmers in the sky.

As we approach the shortest day
there are celebrations
on the hill at nightfall.
The old, the young,
joggers and babies:
people gather at this time.
Little groups stare into the west.
There are drinks and cheers,
selfies and laughter.

Some were born here,
many chose to come.
Some to escape suffering:
all for a better life.

This light,
this smiling throng,
revives the thought
that this, our chosen city
is still open,
welcoming those who come.

The Cliff Edge

Iron railings keep us safe,
here since Victorian times:
but you can climb over.
There's space enough,
to sit and watch the sun go down:
but you're very near the edge.

The cliffs are a magnet for some
who've lost their way, and arrive here,
out of their minds.
Maybe they pause as they hear the birds
and the distant growl of traffic
on its way into town.
There are wildflowers and rare trees
and perhaps a feeling of freedom
now they've stepped over a boundary,
left the old life behind.

We can sense some of this
as we make out the distant hills of Wales,
and the tangle of woods beyond the gorge.
As we shake off the strange impulse
brought on by this place,
the air seems clearer,
the heart stronger.

Christmas Eve

Half past three, the last shops close,
too late now for any more.
All the things that we've forgotten,
didn't need them anyway.
Warm wind coming from the west
low clouds bringing rain not snow.
College Green almost deserted,
just some stragglers heading home.

Such a crowd in the cathedral,
come to hear the season's message,
see the choir in procession;
hear the lessons and the carols.
Lost faith leaves behind a shadow,
habits from a church-going youth.
Swept away the lovely stories
leaving not a shred behind.
Forget the manger in the stable,
(just a mistranslation really,
should have read 'a downstairs room.')
If I can't believe these things,
and after all there's no one there
what is all this for? The singing
and the stories told again.

I'm just looking at the faces,
see that now it's dark outside:
and we're nearly half-way through,
soon be over for the year.
Maybe it was always thus,
people gathered round the light,
glad to shout and sing together
make a stand against the dark.
It's the end, we all file out,
the bishop passes on good cheer.
Raining now, turn up my coat,
head off home back up the hill –
to join the others who didn't need
to make this annual pilgrimage.

On reading *Satan's Kingdom*

Today it rained all day,
not cats and dogs,
just persistent rain from a grey Bristol sky.
It was good to be indoors
reading about the slave trade.
How very profitable it was
for men from these parts.
How the beautiful houses I pass every day
were built from the sale of people
who were taken from their homes
and worked until they died.

Of course I knew all this but
never wanted to think about it.
Some things you hear and can't forget.

There were one or two moments
when the gloom was less intense
owners who appreciated their slaves,
– put up nice gravestones when they died.
Nothing really.

I didn't have to read it,
nobody made me,
I just thought I should know
about this thing, which lies about us
to this day.

Paradise

High on his hill he hears them,
like giants breathing
hot air balloons, struggling to gain height.

Looking up he sees the faces
of excited travellers on their special day.
From high above they wave,
and sometimes he waves back.

Down below they see him
tiny, on his patch of earth.
What sort of life down there?
He knows they wonder,
and when they're flying low,
sometimes he hears them laugh.

Then the updraught catches,
to great relief they clear the ridge.
And there is Brandon Hill
with its fantastic tower,
and the whole of Bristol at their feet.

And the little man likes
the way they move on by,
leaving him his private world
his patch of sky.
And they will never guess
this little space,
hidden from the world –
to him is paradise.

Old Mr Two-Trees

I bought two trees from a man who was
unexpectedly friendly.
He put the little trees in my car, then showed me
everything, very pressing.
Held my arm, standing much too close,
gave me his card and said
Come again: but I forgot.
Often drove that way but didn't stop.
Then I saw the place was sold
trees cut down, houses built.
Now there are families
and children with trampolines.

My trees did very well,
they grew and grew,
but in the end my wife said
They're too big, they ought to go.
They were very handsome and to me
felt like a gift.
But it's true, they blocked our view,
so I've cut them down.
And I thought of that man,
old Mr Two Trees,
the friendly arboriculturalist.

Jeremy

One day, going to a poetry reading
at a cider orchard,
in the wilds of Herefordshire,
my sat-nav led us astray.
You have now reached your destination, she said,
as we faced an empty field.
Jeremy laughed so much:
he wasn't one for electronic gadgets.
And he kept on about it
– it proved a point he liked to make.

I miss his laugh, and encouraging smile,
and his wisdom about all things literary.
So many stories true and false:
and an infectious
fascination with words.
His articulacy – is that even a word?
Jeremy would know.
And what he didn't know
about commas probably
wasn't worth knowing.

All that is beside the point.
We loved his company.
We thought we could go on meeting for ever
and the talk would never stop.

Difficult Stuff in Books

Still struggle with stuff I read in books.
Black Mountain Poets for example.
Lovely to have a copy
left by Jeremy.
But for me it's a secret language,
and it came too late.

Poems full of references
to things I've never heard of.
As a young man I did try –
looked it all up.
But it doesn't mean a thing
it's not my world.

Looking back,
so much has passed me by.
I chose the way I went,
other paths I did not enter.

Yet I love our Black Mountains:
Chatwin and his Black Hill.
I looked for it, *The Vision*, and found it,
a real place, close to my heart.
That's the territory of my dreams.

Reading the Poems of Billy Collins

Today it's raining for the first time in weeks,
so I'm in-doors, looking over the garden
at rain falling on the pond.
And I keep reading, trying to work out
why the poems of Billy Collins
are so remarkably good.

He fools us with his plain words.
There he is at his window, looking out,
waiting for thoughts to slip off his pen
and then at one sitting, out comes
another little masterpiece,
from the most popular poet on the planet.

He came to Ledbury in high summer
and told us his secret.
That man in the morning
the one sitting there by the window
nice and quiet and unassuming
writing down what he sees, then
adding just enough home-spun stuff
to keep the turnstiles turning;
that lovely all-American man of the people,
it's not really him.
He's not so nice and calm and bland –
he admitted it,
it's just a person he invented
and lives with for a few hours each morning.

It seems so easy, the Collins method
but it's harder than it looks,
I just have to keep trying.

Talking to Ourselves

The poet Samuel Menashe lived alone,
celebrated his solitude,
observing himself,
the I of his poems –
centre of the world.
This dialogue lasted a lifetime.
He was one of those whose
main quarrel was with himself.

Talking to ourselves,
we allow the separate souls to speak,
instead of always the single voice.
Scratching open wounds
which life with other people
makes us cover up.
So many voices inside the head:
covered by that old ragged coat –
the familiar, threadbare persona
once adopted
never left behind.
We learn to snatch odd moments,
defamiliarisations,
excursions from the ordinary life,
to visit other worlds,
listen to the silenced song.

It is easier to reach with practice,
the drinker's secret place,
the daydreamer's paradise.

Understanding Poetry

Understanding poetry. He hesitated.
I took a step closer,
anxious to hear what the Great Man would say.
It was rare for him to explain.
In all our years,
I was never sure
exactly what he meant.

We were at a party
had to shout to be heard
I was steering him to a quiet corner
but everyone wanted a word.
They kept interrupting
but I held on and at last we escaped

He smiled, put his hand on my arm,
Let me finish, he said.
Understanding poetry is largely,
coming to see,
that it is not necessary to understand.
I laughed to find
I was still such a long way from land.
Please, I said,
what is this understanding?
Ah, he said, in his warmest, most avuncular manner,
That is something you either know
or for ever it passes you by.
And with that I'm almost sure,
he winked at me.

Last Words

borrowed from Oliver Sacks

A liver full of metastases,
so now I know.
I can give up worrying:
distant foreign wars – I've got no time.
The Middle East will have to get on without me.

Of course I fear the end,
but time's too short
and I have things to do.

My luck ran out, that's all.
Now every day I spend with care,
detached,
floating high above
all that was my life,
spread out far below.
I see at last
how it all joins together.

Everything changes
all the time.
No generation like ours
will ever come again.
Nothing will be the same,
it never is.
I'm left with gratitude
for what has been.

The Trick with Time

Yes I tried Proust, and got quite far,
but it didn't suit me: not my world.
He's such a snob,
with his aristocrat friends:
but I got the magic straight away.
That falling swoon into time past,
opening channels to things long forgotten.
A special faculty and once it's running
you find you've developed a new sense.
As though the past is never lost
and time is just a convention,
something that with this trick
we step outside at will.

Jocelyn Brooke is little read now,
but I got on better with him.
His English scenes cast a spell:
the same effect, only stronger.
This time I got quite confused,
thought he must have known me in my youth
or I'd visited the same places
he'd haunted in his childhood.
I had to check his dates and a map
before I could see it was all just illusion.
This portal now open in my brain.
This is what writing can do.

And why mention these two
out of the wide ocean of writers?
I just happened to read them
when I was young and green
and knew nothing of the world.

Slad

What was there to see?
An old man's picture on the wall
and his seat with a view of the woods;
a special beer named after him
and a cloudy scrumpy after the girl.

After fame and travel he came back
to Slad and the Woolpack.
He liked to sit and drink,
alone mostly,
not wanting talk,
looking out at the village
and the wooded hills,
often damp and misty
with rain coming in from the west.

They've resisted change
want to keep it homely,
but it's a funny sort of shrine:
for a very English hero.
A man of letters from the common people
singing songs from Spain
before the rest of us got there.

Words in Time

Sometimes it seems
poets are ten a penny,
they're everywhere you look.
And I've heard people ask,
What is poetry anyway?

From our window we see them:
over here from Spain,
putting flowers on the grave
of Antonio Machado.
He was driven from his homeland
made it just across the border.
Now the place is a shrine,
and the French love him too.
A thoughtful modest man,
his answer to that question was
poetry is *words in time*,
words that fix our daily round,
help us with our ordinary lives
of solitude and silence.

In order to be really sure
you've got the real thing,
wait until they're dead
then visit the grave.
If their words live on
you'll be joining a queue.

Beyond Words

I've been accused
of keeping things to myself;
hiding my real feelings.
They say it's a thing men do.

Sometimes it's like a disease.
There are things in my head
but for some reason,
they never pass my lips.

But I can change.
I can start saying what I really think;
or write down my thoughts,
get them out into the light.

But I have a problem.
These thoughts,
the ones that become my words,
Where do they come from?

I can see the next word,
and maybe one more, but
after that – nothing; a brick wall.
I can't see what's coming.

I get a feeling that words are there,
being assembled, somewhere out of sight.
I feel them
and can tell that they're coming.

But the question is –
if I don't yet know
what words are going to appear,
who is it that is making them up?

Is it the person I think it is:
the me who I've lived with all this time?
Or is it a stranger I hardly know,
who has a mind of his own?

Palette Scrapings

Scraped off the palette,
applied to a board
a picture decided by chance.
Then more paint applied,
straight from the tube:
put on with a knife, a rag or fingers
You end up with the sea,
a range of mountains,
or bleak moorland under lowering sky.

Strindberg painted this way,
enjoying the randomness
and then he would add in the foreground,
a single flower –
yellow daisy or purple loosestrife.
And since he was poor, (on account of divorces),
he sold his pictures.

I love applying paint
in the Strindberg manner,
but the boards are piling up,
and no one will buy.

Moving On

The Dialogues of Plato,
five volumes, inherited from Grandfather:
but what to do with them now?
Many times I visited him
when he lived at the Parkgate Hotel.
At lunch he would hold forth
religion philosophy old books
Here was the promise of answers,
to the amazing questions of youth.

Took years to discover it was all a game.
Instead of making sense of life –
it probably makes things worse.

Wittgenstein, when dying, after all the years,
confounding opponents, mystifying the world,
still worried he was not understood.
So he summoned Anscombe, Malcolm, von Wright
to make sure they had his message clear
but each ended up with a different account.
So the vision he wanted to share with the world
he couldn't quite manage to put into words.
Cleverer than all, the bravest of men,
he failed, and the game goes on.

Yet there was a answer, philosophers won't hear
that philosophy itself is a kind of disease,
and he was the one to set us free.

He tried to escape several times himself
and his favourite students, he told to get out,
get proper jobs doing something useful instead.

Grandfather's legacy plagued me for years
but I took the advice, and moved on.
Just occasionally there is a slight relapse
and the old enchantment comes flooding back.

In Search of Enlightenment

Visiting the Nietzsche-House
in Sils Maria,
by the lake
in the Swiss mountains at 6000 feet
(clear blue skies, pure air,
uplift of spirit just as promised)
I looked for the stone in the woods
where he sheltered
and was inspired.
A massive pyramid rising up in the wilderness,
– so he said.
His Zarathustra stone.

But I can't find it, and apparently
even though it is now a great local attraction,
it is neither massive nor great
nor even a pyramid.
Just an old rock
worn smooth by visitors,
conveying nothing.

Which reminds me
that this unhappy man,
self proclaimed genius and madman
is as strange to me as the birds in the trees.
Yet still he had something.
In a world without meaning
you can create a dream
from the ruins of your life.

The House on the Green

If there are so many worlds,
2 to the power of 50,
as Stephen Hawking said,
there must be one where we bought that house,
the one on the green,
by the church at Worminghall.

I remember the long straight roads
in that remote corner of Oxfordshire,
and an old motor-bike
leaning against a bench in the workshop.
I could already see myself,
off to the hospital in the early morning,
cutting through the mist rising off the Otmoor fen
and back late on summer evenings
pushing past the cows on the common,
pausing by the church
to speak to the vicar, our neighbour.

In that other world
when we got there, they welcomed us,
'Great' they'd say, 'you've got the money,
of course you can buy our house.'
Not their flat refusal
because they were hoping for a better offer.

The smallest chance deflected us.
So me on that bike in the early morning
was never going to happen.
And we moved on
to a different world.

26 Middle Street

We bought the house from intellectual types,
about to move to Australia —
a circumstance we might have thought about
more carefully.

We found ourselves the subjects
of an architectural experiment
by the great Walter Segal.
His disciples visited
to see how we were getting on.
We had wanted the house so much —
the polished wood, the glass,
the acres of sky in every room:
set in an old garden
with honey coloured walls.
But the roof leaked,
the clever windows let in rain,
and all the heat went straight out.
To the village we were the odd couple
in the house behind the wall.
You can't live on sky alone,
not in Oxfordshire, in England.
Weather became an obsession,
clouds and rain scurrying over
from the wilderness of Otmoor.

In the end,
like our predecessors
we craved a place in the sun.
But on our way to New Zealand

we were waylaid
by a terraced house in the city,
with nice little windows, a slate roof,
and neighbours on either side.

Crete 1962

Germanos they shouted.
Bleached by the sun, we looked like Germans,
the enemy, daring to come back
after all they'd done.
They didn't believe we were English.
Germanos they kept on
At last they smiled.
We were just boys,
they made us welcome.

I remember Heraklion,
staying with Dr Yamalakis – such a kind man,
though we lacked a common language.
He showed us his collection –
Minoan relics given by patients
too poor to pay for treatment.
His wife talked to us in French
about her brothers, up in the mountains,
what they had done to them, during the war.
She hissed as she spoke about torture
and how she hated Germans.
We were eating outside under an oil lamp
but I was no traveller,
couldn't take the food,
fed mine to the dog under the table.
She never knew.

Those Girls

The ruins were still there
long after the people were dust:
their language utterly forgotten.
So the Greeks made up stories
about giants and half human monsters
to explain what they saw around them:
but they knew nothing.
Their wild speculations confuse us still,
as we struggle to make sense
– always of course in culturally sensitive ways –
for example those little female figures,
whose bare breasts have gone round the world,
used now to promote holidays in the sun.

An image like that sets us to thinking
about goddesses and cults
as though such things really shape the world.
When what really changes nations
is the endless restless movement of people,
always seeking a better life,
just like now.

And the girls – what were they really?
Carnival queens, exotic dancers,
maybe snake charmers –
brought in as entertainment
on a hot Cretan summer night.

Meeting on a Road

I saw him standing by a broken down shrine
in the shade of a massive tree.
Dusty, in rags, one hand held out:
I would have passed by,
but he held my eye
and signed that he would speak.

He must have seen me passing on that road before
seen me wondering as I looked at him there,
at his stillness, his calm and
his patience with the people passing by.
He already knew my questions, and answered straight away.

We wear the ochre robe, daub our skin with holy ash.
Pray and meditate and wander place to place.
Give up all attachment, leave family behind
depending now on strangers for our life.
Not seeking death
but giving up all hope for life.
There will be meetings on the road,
but we leave behind
the dust and stone of other men's lives.

He bowed his head, that's all he said.
and though I saw him many times
he never spoke again.

Sol Invictus

The dark towards us now,
of a world turning away.
Earth-light fades,
taking colour from the fields.
Days lose purpose, and time passes.

The year is heading towards
death without resurrection.
Outside the sun hidden in cloud
and gales howl round the house,
leaving the mind all at sea.

And yet we have faith.
And following an older lore
make up the fire and come together,
joining again each to each,
reviving the spirit, celebrating
the shortest day.

We know that life returns
and Earth brings forth again.
This belongs to creatures of the sun:
not cleverly devised
by juju man or priest,
but given to us, here below.

Shinrin-yoku

We humans, for most of our time
lived in the woods without shoes.
Surrounded by danger,
sounds of the forest,
smells of animals.
Always part of a group,
owning nothing, sharing all.

It comes to the surface now
with all this gardening,
the worship of growing things,
the amazing spectacle of trees.
Vestigial longing for the ancestral life.

Comes to me on a beach,
no shoes,
wind on the skin,
bird cry,
distant view of hills.

Nostalgia will eat us up:
the thought always returning,
It was better then.
What if,
what if growing grain, living in towns,
that's when the rot began.

In the cave entrance,
sitting in a circle, talking, eating,
looking down from a high place,
safe together.
Forest bathing – immersion in trees,
the sea, the landscape, wind and rain.
Switching off the irritating little man in the head.

Snow

We wanted snow and when it came
the air was so thick,
trees covered,
our tracks lost and the way uncertain.
We looked for the Buddhist's house
a place to shelter
but there was no one there,
so we carried on into the woods.
It's coming harder now
silent except for the creaking of branches
and my breathing.

Open Door

Sitting by the open door I hear the garden.
Wind in the trees,
sea gulls squabbling on the roof,
and from down the hill,
the clock of Holy Trinity strikes the hour.
I can smell lavender and freshly cut grass.
With eyes closed, I would know where I am,
I could show you around.

I'm asked *How long have you lived here?*
And it's many years.
And will you stay here?
That's what I expect.
I am aware of the privilege
but still take it for granted.
And yet I will lose it all.
Before very long I will discover
how and when it will be taken.
How the body that got me so far
will turn against me at the end.

But why dwell on what's to come.
Today the air is warm,
the afternoon stretches ahead,
and the door can stay open till dusk.

The Scan

The nurse put a needle in my arm.
It'll be you, quite soon, she said.
Then the radiographer checked me out
and began explaining about magnetism.
How the rotation of atoms is affected,
which makes tumours appear distinct.
He demonstrated with plastic cups
spinning them in different directions.
Now come with me my friend, he said.

Inside the machine I closed my eyes,
couldn't bear it, inches from my face.
Like something alive, churning and banging,
delicately moving me in and out,
as if it was thinking about my case.
I distracted myself with neutral thoughts.
Didn't want to dwell on why I was there,
or where this all was leading.

He pulled me out, dazed and shaky,
but didn't speak to me again.
Then the nurse came back and I thanked her.
Just doing my job, she said.
Then I left to find my way,
out to the wet December night.

It was, I suppose, satisfactory.
The thing I had feared was not found.
But I felt a bridge had been crossed,
was no longer at ease with myself.

Freedom

I was out of it the whole of May
spent most of my time sitting.
Not reading, not busy at all
just quietly by myself.
No, I would say, I'm not going out,
I won't be joining you.
I rejoiced to be out of hospital,
free and on my own.
Each day spring advancing
the garden coming to life.
I let the grass grow,
and without my cutting and fussing
wild flowers were springing up.
I said I would never complain
about anything ever again.

Of course it didn't last,
this honeymoon with my life.
As my strength returned
I got back to the old routine,
leaving just an everyday kind of freedom,
I hardly notice at all.
But some of it lives on
in the wildness of the garden.

The Return

When you set out, let it be autumn,
leaves falling, days getting shorter.
There is nothing to hold you now,
you've worked, done your bit,
contributed the little you had.

Leave-taking will make you want to stay
but go now, while you have the chance.
Don't carry much, leave it all behind.
The journey will test you,
you will want to come back.

Small towns beside the sea,
so enticing but unfriendly.
There's no aim but casting off,
leaving all attachments behind.

Walk freely on warm days,
become comfortable in simple loose clothes,
let your body move at its own pace.
It's not a race to the grave.

Let the journey be long and slow,
the way is your own way.
The goal almost forgotten,
nearly abandoned.

Let your mind wander
back to an earlier life,
a light glimpsed so long ago,
back at the beginning.

Winter River

No one here.
Houseboats abandoned,
pleasure boats tied up side by side.
A finely carved stern – like a Spanish galleon
sinking down – half submerged.

Mud under foot on lonely paths
a meadow where the rivers meet.
Mud in the water, brown water swirling
making here a sort of delta.
No one passes,
mist rising
the mist has swallowed up the town,
and time itself means nothing,
on Osney Island, in time of flood.
It's been like this for a thousand years.

Tumbling Bay then Long Reach,
the village of Binsey hidden by willows.
Swans and geese on the common land.
Past the lock and the thundering weir,
the empty ruin of Godstow Nunnery
where Fair Rosamund was interned.
After that the open fields,
the wide sweep round Wytham Hill,
then Bablock Hythe, where the famous ferry,
rests on the bottom
sunk in a flood.

Strange weather for October

Warm and windy but around lunchtime
it was like dusk,
the sky was darkening.

Go outside, he said.
Go and look at the sun.

It shone through a haze
and it was red.
It had a red ring around it.

The Sahara sand, they said.
Fires in Portugal, they said.

But I knew it was a sign,
I just didn't know what it meant.

Summer's End

We thought that summer would never end
but now a season's come when
I must crawl like Captain Oates.
They'll leave without me,
and in the quiet,
there'll be time to think.

I realise now the past is not a film,
all rolled up on a giant spool
each second in a separate frame.

Nor is the train a good analogy,
brief glimpses through the window,
never seen again.

The past is not a place that we can leave
but lives on deep inside us to the end.
Existence so strange,
it's past our understanding
because we're part of this whole thing ourselves.

And still there's that old craving
to believe things past our understanding.

A Secret

Leaves have fallen
and I must rake them up.
And all this symbolism –
the raking and the passing seasons,
I don't buy it,
they're just leaves,
and it's been raining all day.

It's cold and wet, muddy under foot,
time to prepare for winter.
The leaves will rot down to a delicious mulch
and nourish next year's growth.
Even now under the muck
new life is coming.

Hot sweaty work, on a darkening day in late November.
Here outside, away from the sedentary laziness
of housebound life in Southern England.

It's raining harder now, a steady stream,
wind blowing the last leaves off the trees.
I could go on and on
in joyful collaboration with the passing year,
but it's too dark, I must go in.

And the secret:
do you know the secret that makes this possible –
a well fitting, wide brimmed, waterproof hat.

Notes

These are not really necessary but may be of interest to anyone who would like to know more about the background to the poems:

Birdsong The river was the Dee and the house was in Park West, Heswall.

Detachment Peter's father was the rector of St Peter's in Lower Heswall.

On Halkyn Mountain Galena is the natural ore of lead: lead sulphide.

Acrocorinth Acrocorinth is the name of the ancient hilltop town up above modern Corinth. My companion was John Pirie. The extraordinary sight of the sky full of shooting stars was due to the Perseid Shower of 1963.

April 13th 2016 Winston's birthday to be remembered forever.

Last Lunch with Eileen A rhyne is a water channel on the Somerset Levels; 'from Poland': this took place in July 2008, long before Brexit was ever heard of when charming people from Europe were encountered and welcomed all over the country.

The Empire Mr Brown taught at Kingsmead School, in Hoylake in the 1950s. Anti-racism campaigners began calling the empire an abomination in 2020.

At the Hot Gates At The Hot Gates is a quotation from 'Gerontion' by TS Eliot:

> *I was neither at the hot gates*
> *Nor fought in the warm rain*
> *Nor knee deep in the salt marsh, heaved a cutlass*

It is a poem that has been described as antisemitic; I was unaware of that when it made a big impression on me when I was very young. The quotation from Eliot comes from a letter he wrote to EM Forster 10 August 1929: The hot gates – a translation of Thermopylae. I was introduced to this bit of history by reading *The Persian War* (Osprey, 2019) by William Shepherd, an old friend.

Boys Remembering David Verriour who died when he was still a young man.

The Old Fellow The Old Fellow was Harold Macmillan and he was speaking at St Thomas's House – just over the river from the House of Commons.

The Lonely Shore The Nissen hut on Target Road in Heswall, was occupied by refugees from Europe. There is no sign now that it ever existed.

Not getting across the Dee Flint Castle is on the Welsh side of the Dee estuary, opposite Neston.

Attachment Attachment theory arising from the work of Bowlby shows how secure attachments in childhood are the foundation for adult personality. It is one of the useful and humane bits to come out of psychoanalytic theory.

Lost The quote is from Blade Runner: *Attack ships on fire off the shoulder of Orion. I watched C-beams glitter in the dark near the Tannhäuser Gate. All those moments will be lost in time, like tears in rain. Time to die.*

By the Sea Asphodels on the cliffs at Collioure. Raceme is a flower cluster with the separate flowers attached by short stalks along a central stem, and is the title of the poetry magazine started by Jeremy Mulford and Matthew Barton in 2015.

Les Fauves Les Fauves were a group of painters who came south to Collioure in 1905. Their name means literally 'the wild beasts' from the style of their painting.

Elne Elne was once the capital of Roussillon in south-west France.

Sournia Sournia is a village 30km north of Perpignan in south-west France.

Limoges Mr Silvero appears in Eliot's poem 'Gerontion':
  by Mr Silvero
  With caressing hands, at Limoges
  Who walked all night in the next room.

On a Beach The beach is at a place called Los Canos de Meca, south of Cadiz. This poem appeared in *Asylum: Poetry Pamphlet 2* produced in 2020 by The Lansdown Poets in aid of Bristol Refugee Rights.

Goat Years Aphrodite, my sister Katherine's goat, really did enter the *Guinness Book of Records*.

John Remembering John James 21.11.38 - 6.12.15.

Open Day This occurred at Leahurst, the field station of the University of Liverpool's Veterinary School.

May Day Remembering my brother Richard who died on May Day 1989.

The Unexpected Guest The setting for this imaginary encounter is a wedding at Treowen in Monmouthshire, 10.4.2010.

Sheds The saw mill is at Cilfiegan, near Usk.

Being Alone A Welsh mountain poem, set in the Brecon Beacons.

The Trees Oliver Rackham (1939-2015): leading authority on British woodland who said replanting trees is usually unnecessary if not actually harmful: woods will look after themselves.

Assessed under Section 136 Section 136 of the Mental Health Act allows the police to take someone whose mental state is posing a risk to themself or others to a place of safety where they can be assessed – work which the author did for many years.

The Chosen City The year of darkness was 2019 when the country was bitterly divided by Brexit. Bristol was strongly pro-European, but the country was not. Bristol was officially recognised as a city of sanctuary in 2010. The observatory in Clifton is a prominent local landmark.

The Cliff Edge The cliff walk along the edge of the Clifton Downs is a beautiful place, but dangerous for some.

Christmas Eve Bristol Cathedral welcomes all, including non-believers on Christmas Eve.

On reading Satan's Kingdom The book is *Satan's Kingdom: Bristol and the Transatlantic Slave Trade,* Pip Jones, 2007.

Paradise Cabot Tower on Brandon Hill was built in 1897 for the 400th anniversary of Cabot's voyage from Bristol to North America.

Jeremy Remembering Jeremy Mulford 30.7.37-22.4.17.

Difficult Stuff in Books Bruce Chatwin's (1940-1989) *On the Black Hill* is set in the hills on the Welsh-English border near Llanthony and the farm where the story unfolds – The Vision – can be found on large-scale maps. His books had a cult following during the 70s and 80s.

Reading the Poems of Billy Collins Billy Collins appeared at the Ledbury Poetry Festival July 4th 2010.

Talking to Ourselves Thanks to Philip Lyons for introducing me to the poems of Samuel Menashe.

Understanding Poetry Quotes are from TS Eliot, probably.

Last Words Some of these words are borrowed from a statement made by Oliver Sacks (1933-2015) neurologist and writer best known for *The Man Who Mistook His Wife for a Hat,* shortly before he died aged 82.

The Trick with Time Jocelyn Brooke 1908-1966. Best known for *The Military Orchid. The Dog at Clambercrowne* also draws heavily on his life and the Kent countryside where he grew up.

Slad Laurie Lee's village; the Woolpack was his pub.

Words in Time The grave of Antonio Machado (1875-1939) in Collioure, southern France, has become a site of literary pilgrimage.

Palette Scrapings Strindberg (1849-1912), as well as being a famous writer was an amateur painter. Looked down on by serious critics, he still managed an exhibition at the Tate in 2004 – an inspiration for all amateur painters.

Moving On The wars over what Wittgenstein really meant will never end. Gordon Baker (in *Wittgenstein's Method* by Gordon Baker, Blackwell, 2004) produced the radical view that he really meant what he said: that he was trying to free people from mental anguish, to help people make sense of the world. Sadly Gordon died before completing his task.

The House on the Green In 1972 house prices went up so fast that no one would sell; they always thought someone else would come along and offer more.

26 Middle Street Our house in Islip, outside Oxford was the second Walter Segal house ever built. He was one of the founding fathers of the self-build movement. The house is no more, and the little house in James Street, East Oxford changed our ideas forever.

Crete 1962 My companion in Crete in 1962 was Andrew Farmer.

Those Girls Thanks to Prof Nicoletta Momigliano for her talk on Minoan archaeology to the Lansdown Poets June 2018.

Meeting on a Road A sannyasin is a person, usually a man, who renounces material and emotional possessions and takes to the road. This idea has no equivalent in the prosperous west – which makes us look on in wonder.

Sol Invictus The Unconquered Sun: a God celebrated by the Romans on December 25th.

Shinrin-yoku = forest bathing.

Snow A snowy walk at Kandersteg in Switzerland.

Open Door The chimes of the clock at Holy Trinity Hotwells are very comforting but neighbours got up a petition to stop it striking through the night.

The Return This is a response to the teaching of Greek myths by Miss Primrose at my primary school and to poems by CF Cavafy and Theo Durgan.

Winter River The river is the Thames or Isis walking upstream from Oxford.

Strange Weather for October A red sun was seen in London and Bristol, 16th October 2017.

About the author

David Whitwell took up writing poetry late in life as his career as a psychiatrist was coming to an end. He enjoyed psychiatry and yet came to realise how little the theories contribute to an understanding of people and to ways of helping them. He joined the Critical Psychiatry movement and wrote *Recovery beyond Psychiatry*, an early contribution to the Recovery Movement which places the individual at the centre of their care – something that is now accepted as self-evident.

David lives in Bristol and loves being a civilian again. Poetry offers him the chance to explore ideas and feelings free of the old expectations. He has spent the locked-down months at home, cultivating wildness in the garden.

Publications

Recovery beyond Psychiatry
2005 Free Association Press

The Ruins of Summer
2017 Redcliffe Press

Lansdown Poets:
Anthologies 2008, 2010, 2012 and
Pamphlets 2019, 2020